1

Break Free from

Loneliness & Anxiety

'A Powerful Guide to

Overcoming & Creating a Full

Life'.

L Goodrick

Making a Difference

Not all will reach out to friends, loved ones or ask for help from their doctors, but they will go onto a charity's website or phone a helpline to speak to someone to break the isolation.

For every book sold, a percentage of the profits will go to Anxiety UK (anxietyuk.org.uk) and Support Line (supportline.org.uk). Both of these organisations help to give someone else a chance of loving themselves and their life. With your purchase of this book, you are not only creating a brighter future for yourself but you are helping others to break free too.

It doesn't matter who you are or what your situation is, charities support everyone that need them and they only exist through donations. They help millions of people each year and need constant support from us so that they can help others.

Thank you for being an incredible and brave person. You're not just creating a bright future, free of anxiety and loneliness for yourself, but for somebody else too and this act could save someone from taking their own life!

Contents

Introduction Pg.10

Self-Accountability Contract Pg.19

Loneliness, Anxiety and You Pg.23

The Effects of Social Media Pg.51

How Nutrition Can Hurt and Heal Pg.64

Take Care Of You Pg.83

Calming a Panic Pg.100

Self-Love and Self-Esteem Pg.109

Stopping Nightmares Pg.129

Managing Stress Pg.141

Digestive Issues Pg.146

Conclusion Pg.152

Developing your Unique Steps Pg.155

Helpful Stuff Pg.162

Acknowledgements Pg.166

Disclaimer Pg.168

References Pg.169

Introduction

Anxiety and loneliness come in many forms. Just because you're anxious, it doesn't mean that you're depressed and vice versa. Sometimes, one can lead to the other, but it's not a guarantee: someone who is looking forward to a glass of wine one evening isn't automatically an alcoholic.

Do you ever feel so lonely that you want to disappear but, in fact, all you really want is to be found, noticed, loved or just want to feel like you matter? Instead, you feel like you're an inconvenience to others.

In this guidebook, I will give you real skills so that you can get to grips with your feelings. By putting the skills into action, you will reduce your anxiety and have a great set of skills to handle any situation that life throws at you, as well as creating a fuller, and less lonely, life.

Everything in this book is backed by extensive research. But like anything in life, when we start a new skill, the process can feel unnatural and awkward. Regularly practising and putting the study time in, you will become a pro, learning to be present and in control is possible. Don't worry! Everything is easy to do and I will walk you through each section.

I have created this for all of us that experience the crippling effects of loneliness or anxiety. The two may seem unrelated but they can cause each other. You don't need to be isolated to feel lonely; you don't need to have had a traumatic experience to have anxiety. They can affect anyone and at any time and either of them can drain the happiness from you.

Can you relate to any of these questions?

- Do you feel like nobody has time for you?

- Have you ever faked an illness to get out of a social event?

- Even though you have lots of friends, do you often feel alone and like nobody understands you?

- Do you dread going somewhere and feel like you can't cope? Have you ever wished your workplace would burn down so you didn't have to go?

- Have you ever been in a shop and felt like the assistant was hounding you, so you left without buying anything?

- Do you get more pleasure from materialistic items then you do from people?

In this book, I will give you the easy skills to overcome your anxiety and ways to kick loneliness out the window so that you can start living a full and bright future. In the pages to follow, I share my own experiences to show you that you, too, can retake control over your life and enjoy each day.

This isn't your run of the mill self-help book created by a professor, doctor or therapist. I am just an average person that's been through difficult times. There wasn't help around when I needed it, everything took too long or I couldn't make sense of all the jargon out there. As a result, I was left feeling even more alone and was left with even more anxiety.

I share my own experiences of existing in a world where I never felt like I fitted in. I hope that, on some level, you can connect the skills you are about to learn. Not only will they help to reprogramme your mind but actions like simple changes to your diet will help you to feel grounded and in control of your mind and body. One cannot exist without the other.

Many health conditions can cause us to feel lonely and isolated. Then follows the anxiety from the embarrassment. Anxiety can get so bad it forces us to disconnect from our friends or the world. For a large number of people, the pandemic in 2020 caused them to experience some form of loneliness. Simply because your life hasn't been the way you wanted it to be, it does not mean your future will turn out the same. It can be whatever you want it to be. With this book, you'll have the greatness to fill tomorrow with light and love.

I know that your time is precious. For that reason, I have developed detailed, but easy to follow, skills allowing you to get maximum benefit in minimal time and start living the life you deserve.

You will learn:

1. How to control panic attacks and feel grounded.

2. How to make positive connections with people and break free from the suffering of loneliness.

3. Simple dietary changes to help you feel relaxed, sleep better and lower anxiety flare-ups and, if they do occur, they will be mild enough that you still have control.

4. What different types of anxiety there are and how they can be managed.

5. Easy to follow mindfulness skills to stop the negative chatter in your head that hold you back from living a full life.

6. How to love yourself again and enjoy your quiet time without feeling isolated.

Plus, there are additional action steps to help you to fully develop your own methods, to make the skills fit you like a glove.

My anxiety came in the form of being sexually assaulted by my father and his friend when I was aged between 5 and 15. Then, throughout the next 20 years, I tried to cope with the mental and emotional torments that I put myself through. I would sabotage all relationships – it was easier to push others away than to deal with the pain, anxiety and loneliness of possible rejection.

A mixture of small events and a medical condition left me feeling lonely and isolated to the point of trying to take my own life, more than once. Do you ever feel so alone that even your own thoughts are deafening? Can you go days or weeks without seeing another soul and just wish you weren't alone?

I can't give you meaningful encounters. But what I can do is give you the skills and my stories so that you can break free from the isolation that you're feeling. At the end of this book, you won't need anyone to break that desperate feeling in your heart – you will start to love yourself and become your own superhero.

In what you're about to read, I share a problem I had so that you, hopefully, can relate. Then, the proven skills will help you conquer your mental process to overcome that issue. They are all broken down into simple steps and the science is there if you want to read it.

With love in your heart and light by your side. Let's get started!

L Goodrick

Self-Accountability Contract

How many times have you told yourself that *tomorrow.*

you're going to start changing things or *you'll start next payday* so that you will have money to go out and do things?

If somebody constantly lied or broke promises to you, would you believe them the next time, they promised to do something? No!

The same goes for your mind. Just because you make a commitment to yourself, there is that part of you that knows you're going to let yourself down again. What's the point? You know you'll fail, even if it's going well and you've kept it up for a few days, or even a couple of weeks. At some point, you will self-sabotage simply to prove yourself right.

Well, not this time! This is your time to break free: no excuses, no false promises. Imagine how amazing you will feel in a few weeks from now. Your life will look totally different from today. But if you don't take action, then nothing will ever change. Prove yourself wrong for once and become that person you have always known yourself to be.

Holding yourself to your new skills creates self-accountability. You are making a commitment to leave all the self-destructive behaviour behind you and for love to overcome your pain. Having a contract will commit you so that you are less likely to let yourself off the hook.

I ...., hereby agree and commit to take the following steps to hold myself accountable, increase my chances of overcoming the things that have been holding me back and to becoming the person I know I truly am.

I will not let one slip-up convince me that I am worthless or a lost cause. I will respect myself enough to replace the negative chatter in my head with love and kindness. I will find new ways to comfort and support myself when I am having a hard time.

1. I will not sacrifice my own mental health to make others happy.
2. I will not pretend to be something else or think that I have to be what others expect of me.
3. I am giving myself permission to love myself.
4. I will implement the skills in this guidebook and have faith that my being will change on all levels.
5. This is my time to live a life free of hurtful and negative thoughts, attitudes and behaviours to succeed in my life.
6. I *will* love myself.

Signed   ....

Date   ....

Loneliness, Anxiety and You

Loneliness had always been a part of my life from a young

age. I was the youngest child, by 14 years. Even though I had

siblings, I felt like an only child. The environment at home

didn't give me the security and reassurance that I needed

while I was growing up so I felt left out. Often I would feel

like I was only getting attention because someone wanted

something from me or I was causing trouble.

Severe anxiety started to take over my life in my late 20s. I

developed an inflammatory bowel disease called Crohn's.

This was definitely very challenging to come to terms with.

Not only is it problematic but it's also very painful and could

leave me in some very embarrassing situations. The side

effects of the drugs used to control the condition left me

needing a catheter for months and needing to use disabled toilets.

But this book isn't about me; I just thought I'd share a little information so that you know I know how you are feeling. You may not have a medical condition and you may have had an incredible childhood but somewhere down the line something happened and now you're struggling. Whether that's the simple things, like food shopping without feeling anxiety, managing your busy life, looking after a family, running the PTA and your millions of Instagram followers. No matter what your life is full of, you can still feel absolutely alone, and you just don't know how to break free.

These are just a few examples from my life that have caused me great anxiety.

***

One situation, that caused me a lot of anxiety, was going clothes shopping with a friend. I didn't really like shopping for clothes; it always left me feeling self-conscious. We walked into one trendy shop where my friend had picked up a selection of things for me to try on. She stood just outside the changing rooms and, every time I tried something on, I had to get her opinion. I was doing okay until I saw a pair of jeans on the floor that I must have missed. I grabbed them and forced them up to my waist. I thought, "Bloody hell, I've gained some weight, these as tight as hell!" I managed to squeeze into then and walked out to my friend doing a sort of penguin walk! We were both laughing when a man came striding towards me and shouted, "What the fucking hell are you doing?" I felt a hot flush rush from my feet to my head.

The jeans that I had forced on where his. He had taken them off in cubical next to mine, which was only divided by a curtain, and I had scooped them up and put them on! Talk about embarrassing. I can laugh about it now, 10 years later, but at the time I felt sick for days. For the next few years, I did all my clothes shopping online.

***

I used to have to catch a bus from home into the city then another from the city to work. Both bus rides would take an hour so I had to make sure I didn't drink any liquids before the journey or else I would be in trouble. But you know, something must have happened ...

Halfway home from work, my stomach started to gurgle and I felt extremely uncomfortable. I needed to pass wind but, because of the Crohn's, I couldn't trust that it wasn't just wind. The longer the bus took, the more I began to sweat. My legs were crossed and I was hanging on for dear life.

Finally, we arrived in the city and the closest toilet was a good 10-minute sprint away. I had my gym bag on my back and my salon kit over my shoulder and I ran like my life depended on it. Through rush hour traffic and through the busy shopping centre to get to the toilets. I flew down the stairs, scrambled in my bag to find the special key for the

door, rammed the key into the lock and opened the door …
oh no! There was a lady sat on the toilet!

I quickly shut the door, shouting, "I am so sorry!" then fled
to find another toilet. I was mortified and even now I knock
hard on the door before slowly opening it.

***

Another, not so dramatic but still highly embarrassing
situation. I was stood in the queue at the doctor's surgery,
waiting to speak to the receptionist when I noticed my leg
felt really hot. I didn't think much of it and guessed I must
have been stood next to a radiator. The man behind me said,
"Mate, I think your bag's leaking."

I thought, "I don't have anything in my bag to leak." Then I
realised … I must haven't closed the valve on my leg bag
tightly enough. When you have a catheter, you have a bag to
collect the urine and the valve on that was open. I made my
way to the toilet in floods of tears. I must have been in there

for some while because one of the staff came knocking to see if I was okay. I explained the situation and she found me a towel to wrap around myself. A friend picked me and took me to hers so that I could shower and change into clean clothes.

I know this can sound extreme, especially if you've never had a bladder or bowel problem, but most cases of anxiety can give you digestive issues. Later, we will look at digestive distress and the things you can do to ease the symptoms.

***

Have you ever had something happen to you when you were out with a friend and now you avoid that place – or even that friend – just so you never need to worry about them bringing it up?

I once went to a coffee shop to meet a friend. It was a Saturday so, as you can imagine, it was busy. I ordered the drinks while she kept the table. Above the counter, one of the staff had put out a sample tray of muffins. *Perfect*, I thought, *free food*.

It wasn't until I had finished one muffin and had made a start on the second, that I realised it wasn't a free sample. It was someone's dirty plate that they'd returned to the counter. I was so disgusted with myself that I ran out. I messaged my friend, telling her I was unwell. In hindsight, if I had told her the truth, she would have just laughed. Instead, I overthought it and had worked myself up so much that I couldn't tell her until months after – and I definitely couldn't go back to that coffee shop ever again.

***

Have you been in situations where, at the time, it was so overwhelming you had to escape as fast as you could, but now, you look back and realise it wasn't as bad as you thought?

It doesn't matter if you have had lots of small things happen to cause your anxiety or just one major event, like an unexpected bill or a loved one's death, anxiety comes in many forms. But, fundamentally, our body reacts the same way by pumping out the hormones and chemicals needed to help us either escape or fight to survive. Our brain is hardwired to keep us safe from danger and it does that by priming our muscles and increasing our cardiovascular system so we are ready to fight or flight.

What are loneliness and anxiety and how do they coincide with each other?

A feeling of fear or worry that makes a person feel tense and stressed and may verge on the edge of paranoia. This can turn uncontrollable and start to affect our routines. When this happens, it is then classed as an anxiety disorder. The reason we experience the symptoms is because our brain is trying to protect us from danger, whether the danger is a real threat to life or it's our own thought processes that mimic risk. Our brains can't tell the difference between reality or fantasy. The brain sends signals to our body telling it to get ready to fight or flight by releasing cortisol, adrenaline and norepinephrine.

By using a combination of medicine and psychology as well as the skills you will learn in this book, you will have control over your anxiety, rather than letting it have control over you.

We've seen what chemicals are released during anxiety and their effects on our body. But here are 3 hormones that have a positive effect on our emotional state. They create these positive feelings and are important to know because we will be talking about them throughout this book.

1. Serotonin

This gives us a feeling of significance or a sense that we are important among our peers. It also gives us a feeling of calm, accepting ourselves and others around us. When we have low levels of this hormone, it can leave us with low self-esteem, feeling overly sensitive, prone to mood swings, a feeling that we are hopeless, a phobia of social situations and even insomnia.

2. Dopamine

This is our reward hormone. It's the driving force that keeps us motivated to seek out pleasure. As we learn, dopamine is released as a reward and gives us a sense of accomplishment. A lack of this causes us to have less energy, an inability to focus and a feeling of being on a cliff edge.

3. Oxytocin

This is often referred to as the 'cuddle' or 'love hormone' as it plays a role in our bonding with others. It creates a feeling of trust and motivates us to build a sustainable relationship, either as friends or romantically. A lack of this can leave us feeling lonely, stressed and disconnected from the world or relationships.

Do you ever feel disconnected from the world around you or that you daydream a lot?

Sometimes, when we're alone, our minds wander and we can start to overthink things. This can increase cortisol levels (the stress hormone), making us feel anxious. Because we are already feeling lonely, we don't feel like we can reach out and talk to someone. This, in turn, can make us feel more hopeless and we start to questions ourselves with our own negative beliefs.

How many times have friends asked you to do something sociable but you keep declining. Before you know it, they have stopped asking. Maybe you can identify with these thoughts:

- Who the hell would want to be around me?
- I'm pathetic and an inconvenience to others.
- People are only nice to me because they feel sorry for me.

Before we know what's happening, our loneliness has triggered an anxiety response. Our brain thinks it needs to protect us and starts to fire other hormones to get us ready to fight or hide. This can then make us feel like we don't want to go out and mix with others, as we're worried about what could go wrong and then we start overthinking.

It's a catch-22. We feel lonely, which increases our anxiety, then we don't go out in case our fears are real, which leaves us more alone.

Do spend a lot of your time on the sofa or on your bed?

Loneliness can make us feel like we are a prisoner in our own homes. We only feel comfortable in one spot and, as a result, we lounge around in our comfy clothes for more time than we should. Do you ever say to yourself, "What's the point, as you're not going anywhere or no one ever comes to see you? You may as well be comfy."

Do you find it difficult to socialise and interact with others?

I know this one very well. I have often known friends were having fun but they hadn't invited me so I guessed that I wasn't welcome. Just because that's how we feel doesn't mean that's how others are feeling. Your friends may just have thought that you would join them rather than needing to be invited.

A high percentage of people who are lonely struggle with social skills. This could be because they lack confidence, fearing they may say the wrong thing and others may judge them. The more you avoid social situations, the less likely you are to want to go out. Perhaps you have taken something someone has said the wrong way because they were blunt with you and you have spent time overthinking it, taking it out of all context?

Have you been gaining weight?

Loneliness can make us put on weight because we can turn to comfort eating. We are searching out that dopamine hit, sometimes finding ourselves wanting more to drink when we are lonely. We consume things that give us that warm cosy feeling; the more we experience loneliness, the more we search out that feeling. It's almost like that takeaway or chocolate is replacing the need to feel comfort from others. This is one of the reasons that, during the Covid-19 pandemic, so many of us gained weight. Even if you share a home with people, you can feel alone if the people you live with eat separately.

When being alone feels lonely

There is a difference between having a day to yourself and enjoying some time alone and hating the silence and feeling emotional, upset. Loneliness can cause anger or frustration because you wish you had someone to talk to and have a real conversation with rather than the odd message or grunt from your other half. Just because you are around others, doesn't mean that your feeling whole.

Below are the 6 different states of anxiety with a brief description of what each disorder entails as well as how they can be treated through medication, talking therapies and skills that you can put into place to better handle your symptoms.

Obsessive Compulsive Disorder or OCD

This has 2 parts, the first is the obsessions, the second is the compulsions. OCD can range from being phobic of germs to needing something to have an exact place, like an ornament on a shelf; you know exactly where you want it and can't rest until it's perfectly placed. The compulsion comes from needing to eliminate the chatter in your mind. Or, if you have a phobia about needing things to be sterile, you may excessively wash your hands and carry hand sanitiser with you wherever you go and will start to panic if you reach for it and it's not there. It can show, too, as constantly counting money to make sure you have enough for a purchase., These obsessions and compulsions can start to have a huge impact on the suffers life.

How to treat OCD

Medication can help, such as an SSRI (selective serotonin reuptake inhibitors). These are mostly prescribed to help the sufferer manage their symptoms so that they are at a less disruptive level. If medication isn't for you, or you want to try something different, a combination of therapies such as psychotherapy and CBT (cognitive behavioural therapy) could work. Both help to understand how OCD affects you and how a different behaviour pattern can help you to have control. Whichever you choose, be sure to do your own research so that you can discuss with your doctor or therapist which treatment may be best for you. Remember, it's your body and your choice. You may feel that medication plus a talking therapy is what you need.

Generalised Anxiety Disorder or GAD

Do you feel like there is no reason why you feel anxious? If yes, you could have GAD. One of the symptoms if a feeling of restlessness or worrying about something before you have experienced it.

Everyone suffers from some form of anxiety during their life. But it can be more acute for GAD sufferers. They can often feel like they could stay in bed to avoid people or possible embarrassing situations. They can make up scenarios to get them out of awkward situations.

Do you ever have that feeling of dread or being on a knife's edge because a part of you wants to jump into a new situation or experience but the chatter in your head is giving you a million reasons not too? Or you hate being in crowded places. Maybe meeting a friend in a bar, you start to panic and think about what happens if you can't find them and what will others think. This sort of overthinking is indicative of GAD.

How to treat GAD

Rather than an SSRI, your doctor may want to try you on benzodiazepines. You may know these as Valium, Diazepam or Alprolam. They are a type of tranquilliser. Some doctors may want to try you on a combination of one of these alongside an antidepressant. As well as talking therapies, you can also try mindfulness in-between sessions to speed up the results.

Social Anxiety Disorder

This is mostly labelled as stage fright. Have you experienced sitting in a meeting or sitting with a group of people and you've wanted to speak out but you're too nervous about being judged. This doesn't just happen in a group setting: you could be in a one-to-one situation like talking to your manager. If this sounds familiar, then it's fair to say you could have social anxiety disorder.

How to treat Social Anxiety Disorder

Your doctor may prescribe an SSRI or a beta-blocker to increase your serotonin levels. This can help to stabilise your mood. The reason we feel anxious is that our brains are releasing adrenaline and noradrenaline and these chemical messengers cause our heart to speed up. A beta-blocker helps to stop these chemicals and reduce the physical signs of anxiety. In addition to medication, CBT with relaxation skills and mindfulness can help.

Panic Disorder or Panic Attacks

Unlike the others, a panic disorder can purely be related to one particular situation or it could be a symptom of another anxiety problem. Symptoms of a panic attack include heart palpitations, a racing pulse and an intense fear of being completely out of control.

How to treat Panic Attacks

Benzodiazepines and SNRIs (Serotonin and norepinephrine reuptake inhibitors) work by blocking the reabsorption or reuptake of serotonin and norepinephrine into the nerve cells that released them. Your doctor may introduce an SSRI and a beta-blocker. These all work to create balance in the brain. You will need to work with your doctor to get the balance right for you. When you try something new, see how you feel and report back to your doctor. They may want to adjust the dosage so you have a good balance and you feel in control 99% of the time. If you still panic over that 1%, ask your doctor to refer you for talking therapy. A therapist will give you skills to help you to cope better.

Post-Traumatic Stress Disorder or PTSD

This can affect anyone that's experienced something traumatic, maybe unplanned surgery or a car accident. PTSD can be quite common in ex-military or other professions that put someone in extremally stressful situations or environments. It doesn't need to be a major event; it can also be caused by small but frequent ones too. Most people that suffer from PTSD have flashbacks to the cause of their traumatic experience. People with PTSD can also have panic attracts, phobias and depression.

How to treat Post-Traumatic Stress Disorder

An SSRI may be prescribed, like Fluoxetine, or an SNRI, like Venlafaxine. These can increase energy and help to restore your interest in daily life. in addition to psychotherapy, extreme trauma therapy or brief eclectic psychotherapy (BEP) alongside a combination of medication and talking therapies can provide coping skills to manage the unpredictable mood swings associated with PTSD.

High Functioning Anxiety Disorder

This can occur when people feel they have something to prove. This can develop in childhood, when parents are overly critical or when people have suffered some form of abuse. It can leave the person feeling that they are never good enough and they don't belong. A high percentage of people stay busy to avoid their feelings and they doubt their abilities, no matter how successful they become. High functioning anxiety can often go because sufferers become experts at covering up. They are good under pressure and work extremely hard; they have high ambitions, but they still procrastinate and fear failure and fear embarrassment.

How to treat high functioning anxiety disorder

Tricyclic antidepressants may be an option. These work by increasing levels of norepinephrine and serotonin while reducing a neurotransmitter called acetylcholine which can help you feel like you have more control. Benzodiazepines may be recommended to take when you feel your mind is racing and you are struggling to calm your thoughts down. In some extreme cases, ketamine can be prescribed to slow the mind and body down. Normally this would only be prescribed if you were showing more complexed symptoms. Getting enough sleep and relaxation will help, as well as CBT and talking therapies to help you find the root cause and skills to change behavioural patterns.

***

Anxiety can be complex to treat, as you can suffer from one or all the symptoms above. It can take some time to find what treatments work best for you. Everybody is unique. Speak to your doctor about how you are feeling; they'll be able to suggest strategies that can help you to cope. Remember, if you don't feel like something is working for you, speak to your nurse or doctor.

Can you identify with any of these? If you can that's great. It means the information to follow is going to help you become free from what is troubling you and will help you to cope when life doesn't also go to plan. Like everything else in life, the more you practise these skills, the easier they'll become. If you relapse at any time, we can always choose to go back to a skill and recommit.

"Whether you say you can or you can't, you're right."

[Walt Disney]

You always have a choice. You can choose to never take control and blame your anxiety or loneliness for only living a half-decent life. Or you can take control and live a life full of possibilities. We are all created and we all expire. Make sure that between those two, you fill your life with love and light.

If you think this is going to be impossible, remember that impossible says: I'm possible.

Like anything in life, when you look at the whole mountain, it seems scary and hard work. But when it's broken down into manageable steps, you can achieve your greatness. As we move through this book you will see everything has been broken down into bite-sized chunks so that it doesn't become overwhelming. As you work through each chapter, you'll see how easy the skills are and, with each section completed, you will feel proud that you're one step closer to shaking off that anxiety.

The greatest secret to controlling your anxiety isn't control. The more we worry about being anxious, the more anxiety we feel. The secret to breaking free is simply to embrace what you're feeling, understand that it's only the brain doing what it has developed to do over millions of years. If we worry about something going wrong or something bad happening, we act and think in a particular way. Your thoughts are only half right; the other 50% is the complete opposite! Think of all the amazing opportunities you could be missing out on.

***

Your anxiety has done a great job of keeping you safe but now we need to loosen the grip it has on us and start living a fuller life.

Now is the time to start trusting yourself, look how much you've been through and survived already. You are stronger and braver than you think. But to move into your amazing bright future, you need to do things you've never done before or things will stay the same. You need to let go to become someone that will take action and have power over their anxiety, rather than letting anxiety have power over you. I know it's scary; I've been there. I also know that no matter how many books you read or how many inspiring podcasts you listen to, nothing will change unless you put the skill into action.

At the end of this book, you will see that you are worth more than your negative chatter. You need to stop blaming your past, your illness or somebody else for not having the life you want. Changing your life and your state of mind is as easy or as hard as you want it to be.

What is fear? *False Expectations Appearing Real.*

Just because you are expecting your life to be like your past, doesn't mean it's true. Buying this book means you've made a decision that you want your future to be different.

"Action is the Antidote for Despair." [Dr John Henry Bias]

The Effects of Social Media

Is it making use lonely?

A little social media is great. It can keep us in touch with people we like and look up to. But too much use and it can start to take over our lives, just like any addiction. A few glasses of wine are okay but too much and it starts to become a problem. Remember, anything that makes us feel good causes our brains releases dopamine, the feel-good hormone. Because we like to feel good, we start to chase after that feeling. This is exactly how addiction starts.

You may think that you're not addicted to social media so this doesn't apply, but you're wrong. We now live in an age where most of us are glued to our phones and for good reason. A huge amount of people have *everything* on their phone, banking, social media, photos and most will use their phone to send emails and use the Internet to book a restaurant, order takeaways or get directions. All of this is perfectly fine *in moderation.* But too staring at our phones can be destructive to our social skills.

I know. I used to live on my phone, always checking my social media accounts to see if anyone had liked my post. Or I would go onto a messaging app to see if the message I sent had its one tick or two. If he had read it why was it taking him so long to reply? Sound familiar?

Have you ever looked through your partner's friends list to see who it was that liked one of your partner's photos or clicked onto that person's profile to sneakily check them out?

When you wake up in the morning, do you check your phone before getting out of bed or even saying good morning to your partner? Do you ever think your phone has beeped or vibrated in your pockets and you were sure that you had a notification, only to discover that when you check nothing was there? This could mean you've started to become addicted or you're completely addicted and haven't thought about it until now. Do you struggle to get through your day without checking out your favourite social media app? If it's a yes, then this is a problem.

You are distant from your friends and, rather than engaging with them face to face, you now do interact online through social media. It has been proven, by multiple studies, that this causes people to feel disconnected from human contact. We are searching for that dopamine hit through our phones or laptops, rather than spending time with people that are important to us.

I used to do the same until I realised just how much control it had on me and how it made me feel. The more time I spent on the Internet, the more I felt alone, which is crazy because the reason I was there was to connect with others. I remember sitting with my family, the TV on but instead of watching, we were all on our phones totally lost in whatever we were looking at. It's scary but true.

How many times have you been sat in a restaurant and seen someone taking a photo of their meal on their phones? Have you been sat at dinner with someone, only for them to start looking at their phone, instead of you? We feel unimportant and possibly a little foolish.

Like any form of addiction, social media makes us withdraw from our surroundings and starts to have negative impacts on our relationships in the real world. Rather than seeking out our friends for love and support, we turn to social media because we get that hit of dopamine and we can access it anytime. Most of us wouldn't feel comfortable phoning a friend at 2 o'clock in the morning. So what do we do instead … we go onto social media to see if anyone else is awake.

I used to be terrible at checking celebrities' profiles to see what they were doing in their lives or looking at what the next trend was going to be. I would compare my life to others, even though I knew that their images have multiple filters on, or they would only post about how amazing life was and how well they were doing. I knew, deep down, most of what I was seeing or reading was dramatised, to make it more appealing, but I still took it all in. This led me to feel like I wasn't good enough how I was and it gave me a sense of loneliness and isolation.

A 2010 study from Carnegie Mellon University, Pittsburgh, found that when interacting directly with friends on Facebook – whether posting messages or pictures, tagging photos or 'liking' things – an individual's feeling of well-being and sociability increased. But when they passively consumed content on Facebook, the opposite was true. An earlier study from the same researcher found that increased Internet use led to a decline in communication with friends and family and increased levels of depression and loneliness.

Do you think this is crazy?

Back in the early to mid-80s, people would have never thought that all this technology would create so much isolation. In a time where everything is accessible 24/7, we are constantly taking in idealised images of holidays, family life and striving for the perfect body that we all feel we must have. These don't make us feel good; all they do is create negative feelings.

In 2018, a study to determine the participant's mood and well-being looked at 143 people's use of social media. Participants were randomly assigned to a control group, which had users maintain their typical social media behaviour, or an experimental group, that limited time on Facebook, Snapchat and Instagram to 10 minutes per platform, per day. The study looked at 7 outcomes, including 'fear of missing out', anxiety, depression and loneliness. Participants who reduced their time on social media sites saw a statistically significant decrease in depression and loneliness. The control group did not report an improvement.

Social media has made it a norm that 'ghosting' someone is acceptable. Is it hardly surprising if someone was to 'ghost' (meaning to ignore you and block you out of their lives with no or little explanation) one minute, it can lead to self-esteem and self-confidence issues. Whether you have been dating or friends with someone, for months or even years, and suddenly one day, when you message or call them, you then discover that you've been blocked, I'm sure that would leave even the strongest person wondering why.

But in an era where social media is so present, it's easy to block someone and instantly move onto the next person or thing that makes you feel good. This happens a lot on dating apps: swipe left for not interested and right if you are. I know of one app, that is used a lot in the LGBTQ+ community, where if your face doesn't fit, or you're a little overweight, or too slim, you get hate messages. The worst thing about that app is it shows how far someone is away from your location, even to the nearest metre. These apps are focused on how you look, with nothing to do with your personality or your values.

People are no longer polite because they don't have to be. They just move onto the next, leaving people feeling that they're not good enough or that they don't belong. This makes people feel anxious, lonely and isolated, simply because you don't look like how we've come to expect attractive people to look.

When we combine low self-esteem with low confidence, most of us find ourselves struggling to ask for help. We are afraid that others will judge us, so what do we do? We turn to social media or our phones to try and feel better about ourselves. We check and check and keep checking how many likes we get on a post and for new followers. This gives us that shot of dopamine that makes us feel good for a short time. When it's gone, we go back and repeat the cycle because our brain is wired to search out for that hit.

How do we move away from the dependency on social media and reinforce that we aren't destined to be alone or anxious to interact with people in the real world? This will feel like a detox and you may feel uncomfortable at first. At the start, I felt like my hand had been chopped off! It took me a week or two to get over no longer needing social media. You will soon be filling your time with more productive and positive activities.

Don't worry, you will still be able to use your favourite sites. But you will have control over it, rather than feeling like you need to constantly keep checking your devices.

Try these simple steps to break free from the hold social media has over you:

1. Disable notifications on devices. Make sure you remove the badges, sounds and notifications on the lock screen.

2. Remove notifications when you receive messages from the apps you visit the most, be that Facebook, Instagram or emails.

3. Block yourself from sabotaging your efforts. This could be deactivating your Facebook account for a set period, posting a status that tells everyone that you have decided to step away for a while to focus on you. Deactivate the account, then delete the app so that you aren't tempted to have a sneak peek after a month. If you do reinstall the apps, move them onto a screen where you can't easily see them. This way, we lower the risk of becoming readdicted.

4. Move your device out of sight. If you're working, leave your phone in another room or in your bag.

This will help to stop you from mindlessly checking your phone for updates throughout the day.

5. Some phones let you limit your screen time in the settings. If you're using a computer, you can download software to help you focus and limit distractions.

In no time at all, you will start to realise that you are stronger than you first thought. Rather than wasting hours scrolling through social media, take the time to go out for a walk, get some fresh air and connect with nature. Just seeing other humans, you'll feel part of the real world again.

You will no longer feel the need to check to see if anyone has messaged you. If you're feeling lonely, give a friend a call – hearing another voice can help us to feel like we are not alone. Maybe visit a neighbour's house or join a group, either a charity or a church that does a coffee morning is a good place to start. Or join a club. Even taking part in a gym class is great interaction that will help to open up your social circle and will give you a boost in endorphins, serotonin and

our favourite dopamine. All of these will give you a sense of

well-being, calmness and positive connections that will help

to build relationships

How Nutrition Can Hurt and Heal

The more information you have, the greater your power to overcome anxiety and loneliness will be, as long as you take the right steps.

You may already be aware that some foods can make anxieties worse. But do you know why? In this chapter, I will show some of the foods that can make you feel more anxious. Knowing these truths helped me to understand why something had a negative effect on me whereas others had positives and helped me to start taking control.

In chapter one, we found out that certain chemicals were the cause of our anxieties and that some medications can increase or decrease the levels of those chemicals to make us feel better. Food can do the same, helping us to be in control of our feelings.

We know that when anxiety flares, we feel on edge: our hearts race and our minds go into overdrive. This happens because the body is getting ready to fight or run, to get us ready for the danger and to protect us.

The chemicals that control this are:

- Adrenaline
- Cortisol
- Norepinephrine

Certain foods can increase these chemicals, so limiting their intake will not just make us feel better, they will also allow us to make more rational decisions, making us feel in control and reinforce positive feelings. Think about it, you will have more control when you're in a stressful environment or situation just by making some simple swaps or avoiding certain types of food.

Caffeine

Caffeine is found in teas, coffees, energy drinks and chocolates. Don't worry, I'm not telling you to never eat chocolate ever again but reducing your intake will definitely help. We know that having that extra cup of coffee gives us the jitters and helps us when we're tired and needed the energy. But where does that energy comes from?

When we consume caffeine, our body treats it like a toxin that it needs to get rid of. In response to this, our adrenal glands pump out adrenaline, also known as epinephrine. This is where the energy comes from. Simply put, every time we consume caffeine, we are putting ourselves into a fight or flight mode and the more we have, the worse we feel. When we have a little too much caffeine it can feel the same as a flare-up of anxiety. Consumed every day, for years and years, the adrenal glands that produce the hormone will become exhausted. A side effect of this is that it creates a feeling of burn out, which can lead to people thinking they need more caffeine to cope.

By cutting it out, you are giving yourself a huge step up in the fight against anxiety. I know how exhausting life can be and we still want that hit, but cutting down your caffeine intake by half is still going to help.

Here are 4 supercharged suggestions to help give you an energy boost without all the negatives that caffeine can bring. You will have heard of most of them but maybe not realised just how great they are. If you are used to having caffeine daily, when you start to cut back or cut out you may notice that you go through a withdrawal phase. Don't worry, it will pass in around 3–5 days. Drink plenty of fluids and take painkillers if you get headaches.

All the suggestions below also have a positive effect, directly reducing anxiety symptoms.

1. Vitamins

When we are lacking energy, it can be because of a deficiency of certain vitamins. Taking a high potency multivitamin and mineral supplement can help. But if you're continuing to feel tired, you may need a more targeted approach to get on top of a deficiency. The key nutrients you need to focus on are:

- magnesium
- potassium
- B vitamins, including B12
- iodine
- plenty of sunshine for vitamin D

Can't I just get it from my diet? In one word, no! Unfortunately, the way our foods are grown and stored, a high percentage of the good stuff that we need is lost. Take an orange, that we expect to be packed full of vitamin C.

If we were to eat the orange straight from the tree, as soon as we picked it, we would receive around 45 mg of vitamin c. But when we eat an orange from the supermarket, picked a few days ago and then artificially ripened with ethephon, we only get about 22 mg. This is then reduced further by how long it has been sat in the store and sat in your fruit bowl at home, so by the time we consume it there could be as little as 5 mg. All we are left with is water and fibre. It is still important to eat your fruit and vegetables, but supplementing this with vitamins will help too.

There are thousands on the market and they're not all created equally. In the resources part of this book are my recommendations.

2. Exercise

While you may feel like you don't have the energy to exercise, doing just 20 minutes of steady walking can increase the amount of mitochondria the body produces to meet our need. This is what we need to have more energy so, if you're feeling that afternoon slump, try going for a walk in your lunch break or before you pick the kids up. Cardiovascular exercise, like walking, releases endorphins helping to reduce some anxiety. If you don't have time or it's not convenient to go for a walk, you can still feel the effect and get the benefits from 10 minutes of stretching.

3. Water

Drinking at least 8 glasses of water a day will help to flush out toxins that have been stored up in your liver and kidneys. A good flush out may be just what is needed to release the natural energy from our diet. Aim to drink 2 litres of water throughout your day.

Being dehydrated can make you feel sluggish. A study, conducted by Public Health England, found that individuals with mild dehydration and undergoing demanding physical activity, experienced a decrease in performance due to increased fatigue, reduced motivation and endurance. Dehydration is also thought to adversely affect performance because of an increase in body temperature, which then can cause an increase in heart rate.

4. Herbal Supplements

Taking a herbal supplement can give your body a helping hand, sustaining higher energy levels and creating a balance within our bodies. one that has repeatedly been proven to help is Rhodiola rosea, a well known and traditional remedy to help combat stress, depression and anxiety. It works in various ways to modify serotonin and dopamine levels, as well as giving the body a boost of energy. The normal recommended daily dose is 50 mg and a dose of 300 mg or higher has been shown to work as a natural antidepressant.

71

There has been extensive research on the effects of Rhodiola rosea, showing it to be extremely effective at reducing anxiety, as it slows down cortisol and adrenaline release.

(Source – www.ncbi.nlm.nih.gov/pubmed/17990195)

Glucose and Sugar

When we don't consume complex carbohydrates in the form of wholemeal bread or pasta and wholegrain cereals, we can experience a huge peak in blood sugar, followed by an incredibly fast fall in sugar levels. This can make us feel anxious as our bodies need glucose to function. The brain, when it doesn't have enough glucose, can send us into hypoglycaemia as it runs out of fuel. Symptoms include:

- Yawning
- Forgetfulness from slowed down thinking
- A 'foggy' brain
- Dizziness

- Headaches

- Fatigue

- Difficulty thinking

- Blurred vision

When you get these warning symptoms, you need to move quickly and eat a carbohydrate-rich meal to get your blood sugars up quickly. These warning signs mean that your brain doesn't have enough fuel to function. To protect itself, the brain takes glucose from the blood, causing the body to panic. The liver and muscles need glucose to function too so this triggers the stress hormone cortisol and adrenaline. Their job is to raise glucose levels again and this is when we start to feel our anxiety flare. Other symptoms we can experience include:

- Irritability

- Palpitations

- Panic attacks

- Short temper

Feeling Hangry?

When we eat simple carbs, that have been processed or refined, our body breaks them down super-fast, resulting in a huge rise in blood sugar followed by even greater falls. We enter the cycle of our brain protecting itself, followed by our bodies going into fight or flight mode as it tries to cope with not having enough fuel. This is known as 'reactive hypoglycaemia'.

Here are some questions to ask yourself to help you determine if your anxious feelings come from low blood sugars:

- Do you get 'hangry'? Do you feel angry when you're hungry?
- Does your mood fluctuate throughout the day?
- Do you eat a lot of junk food or foods that have been changed from their natural form? Do you drink

sugary drinks? (Even products labelled as 'no added sugar' still contain sugar. It simply means that additional sugar hasn't been added.)

- Do you skip meals? (Going without breakfast is a huge no-no. After we've slept, our blood sugar level is already low and by skipping breakfast, it can become even lower. If there isn't enough glucose to carry out our daily tasks, this will trigger the release of adrenaline.)

- Do you ever wake up feeling anxious? (This can happen because you didn't eat before bed or your evening meal contained simple sugars, such as alcohol or junk food.)

Try to cut out or reduce to once or twice a week treats in the form of simple sugars and processed foods:

1. Biscuits, cakes and sugar

2. White refined bread, pasta, rice, cereals and cereal bars, fruit juices, white potatoes, pizza

3. Sugary drinks

4. Wine and beer

When you first cut these down, like caffeine, you may feel the effects of withdrawal. But again, this will pass.

Try to follow a low glycaemic or a low glycaemic load diet. These will help to stop the high peaks and rapid falls of your blood sugar levels. They are super-filling too and will help to reduce your sugar cravings. Find these online or, if you have a pre-exciting medical condition, your doctor or nurse may be able to provide you with information.

Make sure you're eating every 2–3 hours, even if it's just a snack. Make sure that you have protein, complex carbs and a source of fat at every meal – and a snack in-between if you can. A handful of nuts or seeds or a slice of wholemeal toast with cheese will give you the fats, carbs and proteins to stabilise your glucose levels.

If you're still struggling with cravings you could add in a couple of supplements that help level out your blood sugar levels.

1. Cassia cinnamon

This can be added into smoothies, sprinkled on toast or added to your cereal, porridge or muesli. If that doesn't sound appealing, you can buy it in capsule form. Make sure you follow the suggested intake on the bottle.

2. Chromium

This is an important mineral that is needed for normal blood sugar control and is normally missing from processed foods. It helps our body's to metabolise fats and proteins, as well as carbohydrates. Unlike cinnamon, you will need to take this as a supplement once a day. Chromium is a good one to help the 'hangry' feelings to pass.

We can get micro amounts from a balanced diet and chromium is present in:

- Wholegrains

- Broccoli

- Green beans

- Lentils

- Spices

Alcohol

Have you ever been out on a bender or been at home and polished off 3 or even 4 glasses of your favourite tipple and the next day you felt anxious or a little down? It's common knowledge that alcohol is a depressant but most people don't know that it can also make anxieties worse.

After one glass, our brain releases serotonin and endorphins, which gives us that euphoric feeling. We drink more to keep that effect going. But once we stop, that increase of serotonin and endorphins we had begins to drop and we feel a bit shitty. This is when most people experience low mood and

stressed so our body releases cortisol and norepinephrine ...
Can you guess where this is going?

We start to feel the flight or fight mode and, before you know what's happening, you're sent on that spiral to full-blown panic. You could reach for another glass of alcohol to make yourself feel better and let those feel-good hormones come flooding back. Or you may choose to focus on something that gives you a warm cosy feeling while you wait for those chemicals to balance out. The latter is your best option if you want to get to grips with your anxiety.

We know that drinking 2 litres of water a day will improve energy and helps our brain to function efficiently too. When you have a tipple, have a large glass of water with each alcoholic drink. This will help our body to regulate its self and we can lessen the impact that drinking has on us. Drinking more water will allow the serotonin and dopamine to reach their destinations so that its easier for us to feel in a balanced state. A lack of water also impacts blood flow, which makes our muscles tense, increases our heart rate and we even sweat more.

Here are some simple ways of getting water in while we are consuming alcohol:

1. Add ice to your drinks

2. Drink a glass of water in-between alcoholic drinks

3. Use tonics or soda waters, making sure they are sodium-free

4. Snacking on fruits with high water content, like watermelons, oranges, strawberries and grapefruits

5. Have an extra cucumber in your G&T

Switch to drinks with lower alcohol content and look out for 'light' beers or wines. This will slow down the rate at which water leaves your body, reducing the risk of becoming dehydrated. If these don't sound appealing, have a couple of large glasses of water *before* you start drinking.

If, after reading this, you feel you would rather not risk encouraging your anxiety to flare up, have a night free from alcohol or even give it up completely. Whichever you decide, just make sure you are happy with your decision and know that you're not depriving yourself but actively making a choice to take responsibility and control over your anxiety levels. That is a very courageous and inspiring decision.

Take Care Of You

'Life is a marathon, not a race'.

Taking care of yourself

These tried and tested methods will help to keep you connected to the world around you. Be kind to yourself: eat natural whole foods instead of processed junk. I know junk food tastes good but most, if not all, the good stuff (the vitamins, minerals, essential fats, and fibres) have been taken out and chemicals needed to enhance the flavour or shelf life pumped in.

Make sure you're getting plenty of sunshine. A lack of vitamin D can result in lower levels of serotonin and dopamine, which has been linked to depression. Speak to your doctor about getting your levels checked before you take any supplements, too much vitamin D – or any other vitamin – can be just as bad as not having enough. Simply getting outside and going for a walk in the sunshine will help to naturally top up your levels. In summer, make sure you're not covered in sunscreen for the first 10 minutes so the sunshine can be absorbed into your system.

Good fats, especially the ones coming from fish, have been shown to lower depression. If you don't consume animal products then nuts, seeds and flaxseed oil are also great sources.

One study found that "Omega-3s have been studied in various mood disorders, such as postpartum depression, with some promising results. In bipolar disorder (manic depression), the omega-3s may be most effective for the depressed phase rather than the manic phase of the illness. The omega-3s have also been proposed to alleviate or prevent other psychiatric conditions including schizophrenia, borderline personality disorder, obsessive compulsive disorder, and attention deficit disorder." [David Mischoulon, MD, PhD]

A fascinating clinical study, conducted over 11 years, showed that omega-3 fatty acids provide numerous health benefits, including in a variety of psychiatric symptoms and disorders such as stress, anxiety, cognitive impairment, mood disorders (major depression and bipolar disorder) and schizophrenia. Omega-3 fatty acids may additionally represent a promising treatment strategy in patients with PTSD. [clinicaltrails.gov by the Durham VA Medical Centre]

If you want to read more about nutrition, look at the reading list included at the end of the book. I think you'll be amazed at the information and hope it helps you to make informed decisions. If you're unsure, ask your doctor to refer you to a nutritionist.

Try taking out stimulants, like caffeine from your diet. I know most think of coffee and energy drinks, but tea has nearly as much too. Coffee has around 47 mg of caffeine per regular cup and tea is around 34 mg!

Look out for an energy boost that won't send your anxiety into overdrive. Herbal teas are great but it can take a few attempts to find ones that you like. These are my favourites, they'll keep you hydrated too.

- Ginseng. This herb helps aid your body in adapting to stress and helps boost energy and stamina without caffeine.

- Maca root. This will give you energy in a balanced and sustained way, and it never stresses your adrenal glands (the glands that produce adrenaline and norepinephrine).

- Green tea. This does contain caffeine but it also has an amino acid called L-theanine which counteracts the caffeine. It has beneficial effects on mood, sleep, emotion and cortisol. This can help your body cope with stress.

- Chicory. A great alternative to coffee. Made from roasted chicory root, rather than coffee beans, it even supplies anti-inflammatory health benefits. It can also help to reduce blood sugar and improve overall digestive health.

Other strategies for looking after yourself include:

- Laying in a calming place that's warm. Close the curtains and listen to some guided meditation to calm your mind. Maybe use essential oils, like camomile, lavender and eucalyptus. This is a super-relaxing and clearing blend. Use them in an oil burner or a diffuser or even mix them with a carrier oil and apply them to the souls of your feet. Don't forget to put a pair of socks on so you don't slip!
- Calling someone rather than messaging. Social interaction will help you to feel less alone. Have a list

of 3 people you can call as this will reduce the risk of no one being free to talk.

- Sing! Even if you can't hold a note, play a song that you love and makes you sing along. Grab a hairbrush or wooden spoon and even dance along if you can. Doing this will release endorphins and make you feel great.

- Try slowly cutting back on any addictions. This can seem scary. I used any excuse I could find to hold onto mine. I used to smoke; I felt like I couldn't cope without cigarettes. This is just an illusion and the only reason we feel relief is because they have caused a dependency on nicotine. When we don't have it, we feel the withdrawal and, like any drug, as soon as we have our hit, we feel relaxed again.

Food, particularly sugars, salts and fats, stimulate the same dopamine response in us. The feel-good and reward hormone is the same that we also get from alcohol and cocaine. Once we get a hit of dopamine, we want more. This is where addiction starts. Don't worry I'm not recommending that you give everything up, but cutting back or quitting if you can you'll save some money and you will feel proud that you broke a negative habit. It's a win-win.

I've been there. I know exactly how daunting changes can be. Along the path of 30 years of struggling with my issues around trauma, I developed a dependency on alcohol. At least 2 bottles a day went down easily, plus a pack of cigarettes. I only ate pure junk food. I was obsessed with it all. Smoking, drinking and junk food were the only 'good' things in my life: they were always there for me and would never judge me.

As the years went by, these all seemed to stop working for me. I didn't get the pleasure they used to give me, so then I turned to the harder stuff. At first, it was mephedrone, which I snorted. This is a simulate and it made me feel like I was on cloud 9, all the negative thoughts and feelings I had slipped away. But like anything, it doesn't last forever. Once this lost its effect, I turned to cocaine, which I also snorted, giving me was an intense feeling of being happy. I lost contact with reality and, for the first time, I felt like I could have sex without having all the flashbacks that used to stop me before.

As much as I tried to only do drugs at the weekends, it wasn't long before my use started to creep into my weekdays too. I was a hairdresser and doing drugs was an almost acceptable part of the industry. Obviously not taking illegal drugs at work, but there weren't any hang-ups or disapproval with being open about taking them at the weekend, which meant I could keep hold of my habit until they started to destroy my life.

For people that are constantly struggling to understand their emotions, or trying to process the never-ending cycle of self-destruction, then having an escape and switching off your overthinking or overanalysing brain for a brief time is amazing. But no matter how much we try and avoid the mental torment, it always catches up with us. Our toxic behaviour isolates us even more and, before we know it, we're in a position or have become a person we don't recognise anymore.

I got through it. Now, rather than just living to exist from one day to the next, I'm living a life free from all the negatives. I have 99% control over my anxiety. I no longer disassociate and, if I ever feel like I'm starting to disconnect, I use my pebble and the skills of breathing and reconnecting to my environment. I go back to my checklist to see which positive habit I've come away from. Sometimes, I've consumed too much coffee it has overstimulated me so that I can't sleep. That's when negative chatter will creep in. I recognise this happening and nip it in the bud.

I still have sugar and fat; I enjoy having treats and there is nothing wrong with that. I enjoy the odd glass of wine too. I'm not perfect but I know how my anxiety and PTSD works

– it wants me to escape instead of trying to cope. I step back, listen to what's happening and accept I'll never be perfect because perfection doesn't exist. I know, with 100% certainty, I will never go back to the toxic habits again.

This didn't happen overnight. I took it one day at a time and even that was too hard sometimes. Rather than trying to be good for a week, I tried to stay off of the toxin for a day. When that failed, I broke the day down into smaller and smaller chunks. At any goal I achieved, I would reward myself with love, congratulating myself on how well I had done and reminding myself that I am stronger than I had previously thought. By being kind to myself, with positive thoughts and feelings, my smaller chunks eventually turned into 6 months. This doesn't mean I'll never take something into my body that's toxic ever again; I know I will fail with something. The important thing is to always remember that with every failure, we learn something.

If your mood is on a tipping point – one minute you're fine, the next moment you're feeling low – this can be a good indicator that your body could be low on serotonin. Although we can't get this from food, we can get the amino acid that's needed to create it. It's important that we eat foods rich in an amino acid called tryptophan. Serotonin helps to stabilise our mood. It also helps us to control our frustration and aggression levels, improves our memory and can even help ward off addictions. The foods below contain the highest amounts, reducing as you move down the list.

1. Cow's milk
2. Canned tuna
3. Turkey or chicken
4. Oats
5. Nuts and seeds
6. Wholewheat bread
7. Dark chocolate

How to reinforce positive habits and feelings

I found that a great way to cope with my emotions is using meditation. This allows my brain to sort through the junk that I don't need. Doing this before bed helps me to control the nightmares that I used to have, often flashbacks of traumatic times.

I found that a mix of medication, talking therapy and hypnosis sessions all had a positive impact on my recovery from the addictions and help me to cope in situations that trigger my flashbacks. I followed this combination of treatments for a couple of years and, after my talking therapy ended, so did my hypnosis. I felt great. "Why should I carry on with the hypnosis?" I thought. But hypnosis, like any other treatment, needs to be part of a regular routine or else the negative thoughts start building up again and, before I knew it, my triggers were taking over my life again.

Medications helped with balancing out how I felt and they stopped me from having dark thoughts and feelings. But they also muted my happiness in life. I just didn't care much about anything, including 'normal' social interactions.

If you don't use it, you lose it. This is applied in fitness – if you stop running for a few months, you start to lose the benefits of that exercise. It's the same for retraining the mind. You don't notice any changes for a while then, without realising, you're back to hating yourself or having negative chatter in your head. The cycle of suffering begins again. For me, this would go on until I realised what I was doing and then I would go back to the hypnosis.

The reason I stopped going to sessions is simply that I couldn't afford to keep it up. Hypnosis is a trance-like state with a therapist. You sit or lay in a safe quiet room, your eyes closed. The therapist talks you through different stages of relaxation, giving your unconscious mind suggestions to help you to cope with things that cause you stress. Often, these suggestions are positive ways or guided dreams to help give your mind new ways to cope. If you feel that hypnosis would help you, I would highly recommend that you go through a healthcare professional. They can direct you to someone that specialises in your particular issues.

If you don't yet feel comfortable talking to a professional, try looking on the various mental health charities' websites for more guidance. If, like me, you cannot afford private hypnosis sessions then meditation could be a good fit. They are, fundamentally, both working on changing the patterns of your thoughts and the connections to emotions. While hypnosis has a person guiding you through the visualisations or directing the images in your head, with meditation you're alone to guide your thoughts. You can listen to recordings to help you to focus your thoughts.

The advantage of hypnosis is that if things become distressing, a therapist can help you to process your thoughts before the end of the session. This will often involve doing some grounding exercises to allow you to reconnect with the present. You can still get benefits from meditation. At first, be sure to listen to guided meditations to focus, rather than letting your thoughts run away to something traumatic or negative. Start with just 15 minutes and have your pebble ready or the breathing skill to hand, just in case you need them. Once you can do this 3 times a week, gradually increase your sessions to 30, or even 45, minutes. Do what feels right and safe for you.

You may have heard of people meditating, sitting quietly alone with no guidance, being able to clear their minds and feeling calm and collected. This isn't so great for people that have PTSD: our minds can let doubt, guilt or fear creep in easily and so this can have the opposite effect, leaving us with a negative experience.

Whichever you try, make sure you have something to help you to reconnect afterwards.

You can find free, guided meditation podcasts online or watch videos on YouTube. Find something that feels right for you. I love listening to Lisa Nichols, Nick Vujicic and, if you have a faith, look into a support network online. I often listen to inspiring Christian meditations too. Whatever you find, remember to start small and build your time up. There's no rush and it's perfectly normal for it to seem weird at the start. The more you do it, the easier it'll become.

Look at the reading list at the back of this book for web addresses to help you get started.

Calming a Panic

Reconnecting and grounding

How to reconnect and reground

When I first started talking therapy, I really struggled to connect in the sessions. At the start, whenever the therapist asked me questions about my trauma or the things that had happened in my life to make me disassociate, it was easy to talk. It was like I was explaining someone else's situation rather than my own. But then, I would have trouble remembering what we had talked about previously. Other times, I couldn't speak at all. It was so frustrating; I just wanted to make progress and not feel like I was wasting my therapist's time.

The skills below worked well for me when I have been in triggering situations and I've needed to reconnect. All your feelings are normal and a high percentage of people in a similar position have similar experiences. There isn't a right or wrong way to feel.

1. Try and notice objects around you. What colour are they? What shape is the object? Are there any details on it? This will start to bring your awareness back into the space that you are in.

2. How do you feel? Are you hot or cold? Are you hungry or thirsty?

3. What can you hear? Can you hear cars, or birds or even a ticking clock?

4. Try wiggling your fingers and toes. Next, move your head from side to side. Can you feel the ground? Notice the pressure under your feet or the chair you're sat in.

Now that you're becoming aware, know that you are in control. You may need to practise these steps 5 or 6 times while you are present in the moment to recall them when you need them. Having them stuck on a bathroom mirror or on the inside of a kitchen cupboard will help you to remember the steps too.

5. Keep something small in a coat or trouser pocket, or an easy access pocket in your bag. When you feel yourself disconnecting, reach for it and hold it in your hand. Notice its texture. Is it smooth or rough? Play with it or squeeze it.

I always have a crystal in my coat pocket, just in case. I have a variety of different shapes; some polished, others not. They can be something special or pebbles from the garden. A friend of mine uses an old farthing.

Don't forget to breathe slowly and deeply. To make it more powerful, link it with looking into a mirror into your own eyes. I've done this in a coffee shop bathroom and when I've been on a train. I've even used the camera on my phone, just remember to flip the or the camera around so you can see yourself. The more you practice the more you'll become a pro!

If you feel your heart is racing and you feel like your panicking, try slowing down your breathing. After therapy sessions, I was left feeling disconnected from myself and the world around me. I felt as if I was in a bubble. My therapy sessions were held in the town centre and I could easily feel confused and scared. I would walk endlessly around, not knowing what I was doing. I will not leave you feeling that way. Box breathing is an amazing skill to have and will help you in any situation, either to prepare you for tough times ahead or to help you take stock afterwards.

How to Box Breathe

1. Start with sitting or lying down, whichever is the most comfortable for you

2. Take a slow deep breath in for a count of 4

3. Hold that breath for 4 counts

4. Now breath out for a count of 4

5. Wait for 4 counts before repeating steps 2–5

Do this at least 5 times, longer if needed.

If, after doing this, you're feeling low, put on your favourite music. Anything that makes you want to sing and dance is the fastest way to shift your emotions.

Be proud of your achievements. Even if it takes you multiple times to grasp the breathing exercise, just practising the steps will have a positive impact on your life, even if you don't feel it working straight away. The more you do it, the deeper it's going into your mind.

Now it's time to be kind to yourself and celebrate what you have just done. Do something that makes you feel loved and recharges your soul. It could be spending time with your pet or being present with your kids. Personally, I reward myself with a treat night and a movie that'll make me laugh, or spending time with someone that I love. Try not to reward yourself with treats that could have a negative response later on, such as alcohol or drugs.

Be kind to yourself.

The breathing skill can be used in some extremely volatile and highly stressful situations to calm and control your flight or fight mode.

If you've ever wondered how a firefighter has the courage to go into a burning building, you can bet they've used box breathing to control their fears and overcome their bodies natural responses so that they are in full control. They're trained for these situations but if they let their emotions take over, all that training is out the window as their bodies go into the primal mode of fight or flight. Our bodies react to what's going on in the mind, whether it's a real threat to your life or it's all in your head. The brain can't tell the difference. So it does what it needs to protect us.

Before I learnt how to control my anxiety through breathing, I was taking large doses of beta blockers just to be able to leave my apartment to take the rubbish to the bins. In fact, my panic attacks were so bad that I didn't leave home for over a year. Learning to box breathe allowed me to feel in control in the small situations that would normally cause me to panic. Being able to go for a coffee with a friend, for instance. Don't get me wrong, I still had my moments, but they were few and far between now. After a good 3 months, I was able to come off all my anxiety medication, with supervision from my doctor, and I could return to work.

Speak to your doctor before changing anything. They may be able to give you a support network or suggest alternatives for you. For me, I needed to come off beta blockers, antidepressants and sleeping pills for my own sanity. They just left me feeling like I didn't know what day it was, or which way was up or down!

Self-Love and Self-Esteem

Building you back

Self-love should never be overlooked. Relationships don't work unless you love yourself too. When you're in a relationship, of any sort, and you don't love who you are, you're simply measuring your worth by someone else's. *Always* love yourself first. This way, you grow together. If you want to improve yourself, do it for *you* and not because you think someone will love or like you more.

At some point, you'll regret changing yourself for someone simply to fit in with what you think they want or need only for that person to not give you the feeling of love or respect you think you deserve. So, love yourself first. Do what you want for yourself and nobody else. Everything else will follow: your relationship with yourself and others will grow stronger and your life will become full of love and respect.

How to Build Self-Love and Self-Esteem

When we go through traumatic experiences, we get to a point where we don't feel empathy, either for ourselves or others. This can mean we don't understand emotions and cannot empathise when others are having distressing times. This can make us seem like we are hard-faced or that we don't care. This isn't the truth; we just don't have the same self-awareness as others because of what we've been through.

I didn't know who I was or how to make sense of any of the deep pain that I was feeling. My thoughts and feelings confused me: I felt I didn't fit into this world. This often left me being isolated. In an attempt to make the most of my life, I would copy the behaviour of people I looked up too as they seemed to have their life sorted and they had the things I desperately wanted. They had meaningful friendships and loving relationships, wanting the best for their partner, supporting them and building a life that was safe and secure. Copying seemed like a good plan for a 'normal' life … right? No matter how hard I would try, I always had that negative chatter in my head that was saying:

> "You'll never be good enough for someone to love you."

> "You will slip up and people will see you for who you really are... a failure."

> "People only invite you out because they feel sorry for you."

> "Others are only being nice as they want money or free work doing. They're pretending to like you and, once they get what they want, you'll be alone again."

This led me to self-sabotaging. I didn't have the love or respect for myself to fall back on the self-validation that I was good enough and I do deserve to have a positive life. Not respecting myself for being brave, kind and a good person, I would go down the route of a toxic spiral to block out these hurtful thoughts then I would become defensive when I was with others and say things like, "If you don't like me as I am then you can do one." But this was me reacting to the negative chatter that had convinced me that I was a hindrance to others.

Or I would come out with, "You only want me for what you can get out of me." This wasn't just hurting me even more but was hurting others around me too. If they really did want to spend time with me, they sure didn't now.

This behaviour stayed with me for 30 years. As a result, I didn't keep friends for very long. After we parted ways, I would just move onto someone else because I lacked the ability to connect with how someone else's feelings. I was so disconnected from my own emotions that I found it easy to move on and not look back. My life didn't start to change until I could love myself, knowing that I am worthy and that I am damn proud of surviving the trauma I had been through.

In this section, I will help you to build love and self-worth. The skills are super-easy, they just take practice to become a pro!

First, we need to figure out who you are. The easiest way is to ask the people that love and respect you and trust their replies.

Any negative feedback you get isn't really negative. In fact, it's the complete opposite. It allows us to see how we can correct something that we weren't aware of.

Only ask the people that you know won't lie or sugar coat the truth. This way, you will believe what they say – even if you don't yet believe it. These simple steps will help you to see your greatness. Positive feedback will give you an immediate sense of self-love and how much you are loved!

Who am I?

Part 1

Use the example below to write your own message.

Hi, I know you are busy but when you have some time spare, I really would appreciate your help, could you answer these questions about me, please.

1. How do you see me? Who is (put your name here)?

2. Why should someone trust me?

3. What makes me different from your other friends and loved ones?

Please be kind but brutally honest, I love and respect you and thank you for your help.

Part 2

Make a list of all the positives. Then, on a separate page, write down any negatives. Try not to overthink the negatives – remember, nobody is perfect and everyone has imperfections! Negatives are positives in disguise. Now that we know what they are we can work on them to be your strengths.

Here are some examples of the replies I received.

From Amy,

Who am I? Lee, you are loyal, kind and I know I can always trust you.

Why trust me? You always speak your mind when I ask you too and you tell me the truth without offending or needing to be harsh. You never gossip or talk about other people's problems and I know I can tell you anything and you will never judge me.

Why am I different? You never pretend to be something that you're not. My other friends fall into categories whereas, with you, I can talk about anything and everything, from my skincare to my child's poos. There's never any judgement and you just take everything in your stride.

Negatives? You take on other people's bullshit and you can get bogged down by their emotional baggage. You can also shy away from phoning me; you always text.

(We are in the middle of the pandemic so we can't meet.)

Part 3

Now to break these down into easy bite-sized chunks:

> 1. I am always honest and true to myself and others. I am authentic.
>
> 2. I care about people's feelings and I never judge. I am trustworthy and respectful.
>
> 3. I love my friends so much that I let their negative feelings affect me. I need to schedule 30 minutes at least once a week to speak to Amy rather than just messaging. I am a great listener but need to take time away to protect myself.

Try to look at what your 'negatives' are. How have protected you so far? Accept them for what they are and try to leave them in your past

If you received a comment like: "You're always angry" or "You're lazy", think about what is behind that. Are you angry because you are scared of something and this is the only way you know how to react to stop yourself from being hurt? Or are you frustrated with something and you find it hard to process how you are feeling?

Take some quiet time to reflect. Go for a walk and let your mind tick over. You may be surprised that the answers just come to you. Once you have worked it out, think about how you can change. Tell your loved ones why you have this trait. Communicate how you are feeling, remember to use the breathing skill to stay calm and relaxed so you can take the time you need to explore your 'negatives'. These are actually diamonds in the rough: once you understand them, you can turn them to your advantage.

Do this at your own speed, whatever feels right for you. But don't wait until you feel comfortable – nobody likes to feel uncomfortable, but this is where change comes from. Like when you exercise, it takes you out of your comfort zone and may even cause you pain. But if you stick at it, you'll become strong and have a feeling of achievement. Diamonds start life as rough pieces of carbon. With stress and pressure, they transform into rough diamonds. These are then polished so that they can shine and sparkle.

Your negatives are that piece of rough carbon. With the pressure and stresses you feel when you start to look at your negatives, your understanding starts to change, and you can change them into a rough diamond. With patience and practise, they become your shining new positives.

You might not believe all the positives yet but you will. You just need to turn them into bite-sized chunks and repeat them every morning and evening. An easy way of doing this is by writing them on sticky notes and putting them on the bedroom ceiling so that they are the first and last thing you look at. Or stick them around your home where you'll see them often or, if you live with someone and don't want to explain yourself, write them in a text message and send them to yourself. This way, you'll see them often and they will work their way into your subconscious within a week or so. You, and others around you, will notice you becoming more positive about yourself and the things that were negative will become your new positives.

Send out as many messages as you like. I would only send 2–3 out, just so that you don't feel overwhelmed. If are struggling to think of anyone you can send a message to, try using my beliefs about you. I know, without any doubt, that you are:

1. Brave

2. Determined

3. Courageous

4. Unique

5. Resilient

6. Talented

7. Kind

8. Amazing

How do I know this? Because you are reading this book! That means you are a survivor and anyone that has gone through what you have and can still be here is ready to start living the life you've always known you deserve. Clearly, you are brave and resilient, or else you wouldn't be here. You are determined, courageous and unique because, if you weren't, then you wouldn't want to change your situation. You're talented at surviving and you are kind, gentle and always amazing which is why you have someone in your life that loves and respects you.

Self-Love is the Cure to Self-Hate

When you learn to love yourself, you will stop hating everything that you are not and only love what you are!

When you can love yourself, you are also giving others permission to love you. We are showing people how we want to be treated when we go out into the world and when we come into contact with others. How we present ourselves lets others know how we want to be treated. Whether that's to show you love or to hurt you.

When you learn to love who and what you are, you won't need others to like you because you'll love yourself enough to not need reassurance from someone else. You are enough. Feeling love for yourself is an amazing and comforting experience: you will be able to enjoy your own company, which is freeing.

Loving who you are has nothing to do with material things. It doesn't matter how much money you have in your bank account or what car you drive or whether you are in the public eye. These things are nice but if you don't have self-love, your mind will just find a way of being negative. You'll always need more and will never feel satisfied because you will be reaching for the next thing, saying things like, "Once I lose weight ... Once I have clear skin ... then I will love how I look," or "If I were better looking, someone would love me."

Once you have love for yourself, these things won't matter. You will no longer need to be around certain people or be in a particular environment to know that you are worthwhile. You will no longer need that toxic person or that addiction you've been holding onto so you feel validated. I used to do anything to hang onto dead relationships. It became hurtful and abusive and I would rather have felt pain than nothing at all. When you truly love *yourself*, you can finally break free from whatever has been holding you back.

Love brings with its belief, self-worth, value, respect. You'll start to look for your purpose in life: we all have a reason for existing, even when you can't clearly see why. And we always have a second chance to make a fresh start. If we weren't so kind to ourselves today, then we have a chance tomorrow. The sun will always set and will always rise.

How to build self-love and self-esteem

I know that the above statement can sound hard, even impossible. But finding your love is easier than you think. You're already doing incredibly well, trust me. I can honestly understand that after trauma it can be hard to feel like you're worthy or deserving of love. But you absolutely are and with these easy-to-follow steps, you will soon feel your heart fill.

1. Be kind to yourself. Eat food that nourishes your body. Eating over-processed foods isn't a 'treat': it'll just make you feel rubbish afterwards.

2. Spend time with people who help you to feel good. Enjoy their company and relax. Let their positive vibes fill you up.

3. Avoid or limit your time on social media. It can set off that negative chatter. Instead, watch a movie you love and that makes you laugh.

4. When you receive a compliment from someone, look them in the eye and accept it. Remember to say "thank you."

5. Tell others what you like or love about them. Not only does this make them feel good but it also makes you feel good. Your heart opens to receive loving words back and that positive thing you've just done will help someone else to feel positive about themselves. This will leave you knowing that you are a good and kind person.

6. Listen to healing and reassuring guided meditation.

I told you it was easy! You may feel a little uneasy with some of the steps but the more you do them, the more natural they'll feel.

What is self-esteem?

Self-esteem is knowing your self-worth and your ability to be good at something, such as your job or knowing that you are a great parent.

"The self-concept is what we think about the self; self-esteem, is the positive or negative evaluations of the self, as in how we feel about it." [Social Psychology by Eliot R. Smith, Diane M Mackie, Heather M. Claypool.]

If you have low self-esteem, you'll feel like you're not good, smart, or talented enough and will generally have a low opinion of yourself. This isn't something that we are born with: it's learnt from our interactions with the world, either through situations or how someone treats us.

Positive interactions come from:

- Love
- Positive encouragement
- Real love

- Being told your good points

- Celebrating your accomplishments

Negatives come from the opposites:

- Not being loved or false love

- People making a joke of you.

- Never being encouraged or praised for a job well done.

- Pointing out your weaknesses or comparing you to someone else

- Treating you like you don't exist.

Knowing this gives us the power to change the negatives that are coming into our awareness. The more we can step away from them, the more our positives will take over and the more you practise the skills in this book, the more they'll stick. After a short while, you'll be able to be around negative people and it will no longer affect you in the same way. Don't worry, you're already building positive self-esteem just by doing the Who Am I? skill.

Don't forget to celebrate your victories!

The more you practice, the easier your new skills will become. You have chosen to have a great life, full of everything you desire. If you haven't realised by now: it all starts with *you*.

Stopping Nightmares
Reprogramming your mind

For anyone that's been through something traumatic, nightmares are extremely common. These horrendous dreams can make anxiety worse and often leave us feeling in a state of panic, both in the dream and when we wake. For most people, the nightmare is repeated. For others, the theme may change but the sequence of events may stay the same.

You may try to avoid sleeping to avoid the never-ending trauma that your mind forces you to relive. If you feel able to, I would recommend seeing a specialist trauma therapist.

Some causes of nightmares include:

- Medications

- Physical pain

- Eating too close to sleep

- Not reducing blue light an hour before sleep

All of these can cause stress and overstimulate causing the mind.

To overcome your nightmares, we need to retrain your brain. This can be done using dialectical behaviour therapy (DBT) which is designed to help you manage painful emotions. The skill below is based on exposure, relaxation and rescripting therapy (ERRT), a cognitive behavioural treatment for trauma-related nightmares.

The practice of DBT includes 4 behavioural techniques, helping us to accept the trauma. This is done through mindfulness, distress tolerance, emotional balance and interpersonal effectiveness.

- Mindfulness: the practice of being fully aware and present in the moment.

- Distress tolerance: how to tolerate pain in difficult situations, not change it.

- Interpersonal effectiveness: how to ask for what you want and while maintaining self-respect and relationships with others

- Emotional balance: how to decrease vulnerability to painful emotions and change emotions that you want to change.

A 2011 study, conducted at Sleep Med, looked at 47 patients that suffered nightmares due to traumatic experiences. After two therapies were conducted, the quality of the patients' sleep significant improved. The patients also reported an improvement in physical health, anger issues and overall quality of life. The therapies also decreased anxiety symptoms that were caused by post-traumatic stress. The results also showed that a combination of these therapies helped patients to stay symptom-free for up to 6 months.

We are going to rewrite your nightmare and retrain your brain to handle the traumatic experience that keeps playing out in your dream. It's a simple process but takes practice to master, just like anything new.

You will need:

1. A couple of sheets of paper and a pen to make a script as if you were writing a play for someone else to read.

2. A piece of guided meditation music that you find relaxing. This will help your body to relax as well as your mind. (Find suggestions at the back of this book.)

3. Choose a recurring nightmare. Give this a title as you be using this to create a script. If you don't have a recurring nightmare, use one that has the same theme, such as being restricted, chased or exposed in some way.

4. Try and include as much detail as possible in your script. Make it easy for a stranger to understand. Write the playscript and act it out, making sure to include:

- What you see

- What you hear

- Any smells

- How it makes you feel: angry, scared, unhappy, etc.

- Are you alone? If not, who is with you?

- How you are dressed

- How did it start? How did it play out? How did it end?

5. What was the worst part of your dream and how did it make you feel?

6. When you woke from your nightmare, how did you feel? Were you disconnected from your surroundings? Did you feel like the dream was real

and you struggle to tell the difference between reality and your dream-state?

Once you have all this information down on your piece of paper you will need a fresh sheet so that you can write down how you want your dream to go instead.

> 7. Write down what emotions you *do* want to feel. For instance, if you wrote on your first sheet that you felt angry, replace that with you feeling calm.

Here is an example of my own nightmare:

Many years ago, my mum was taken to hospital because she had, what I thought, was a bad chest infection. I had never known Mum to be ill; not even a cold. This led me to believe that she would be okay.

A few hours later I received a phone call from my sister. She was calling to tell me that the doctors had discovered that Mum had heart failure and they needed to keep her in for a few days to manage her condition.

The next day, I went to visit her. While sat at Mum's bedside, she started to go into cardiac arrest. My siblings and I were taken to a side room while the doctors looked after Mum. What seemed like hours later, a doctor came into the room to tell us that they had found a pulse. Before I could hear the rest, I was out of there, straight to her bedside.

I was expecting to see machines around her like I had seen on TV. I knew she was alive; the doctor said she had a pulse. But when I opened the curtain, she had passed away. I was in absolute shock. Why did they say that she had a pulse when she couldn't have?

My nightmare was always focused on Mum being alive. There was never any explanation as to where she had been, but she was alive and healthy. She would sometimes tell me that she had been on holiday for a year and that's why I couldn't call her. I would feel distressed in my dream. Why would she go away for so long and not tell me? Why couldn't I call her? I felt betrayed and angry that she did this.

The dream would make me experience huge amounts of panic. I would disconnect from what was real and what was a dream. When I woke, I would pick up my phone to call her, reliving the pain in my dream again. For the rest of the day, I would disassociate from the fact that she had died and a part of me felt like she was on holiday. My nightmare wasn't just affecting me while I was asleep but while I was awake too.

The worst part of my dream wasn't that Mum had died but that she was alive and hadn't told anyone that she was going away. In my dream, I felt angry towards her because of this and then confusion as to why the doctors had told me that they had found a pulse.

The worst emotions, however, were regret and panic. I would have preferred her to have told me that she was going away, then I could have told her I was going to miss her but at least I would have understood why she had left. My regret was that I hadn't said my goodbyes and told her I loved her.

I felt panic because she had left before I had the opportunity to tell her this.

In reality, I know that she knew I loved her. If she hadn't been so ill, she would have fought for her life, but her heart was too weak. After I discovered this, I no longer had that nightmare. Years later, Mum would appear in my dreams but I no longer suffered because of them. Rather than feeling disconnected from my reality, I woke to feel loved and calm.

I changed regret to acceptance that she had left so fast and it was out of her control. I should tell the people I love how I feel about them while they are in my life, rather than never telling them, then feeling I've been cheated out of that when I am no longer able to say.

Now go back to step 4 and rewrite how you want your dream to play out, replace your negative emotions with positive ones. Connect with the true reasons you're feeling this way. Go over step 7 again.

- Do you wish you could have reacted differently?

- Is there something that you have left unresolved that you need to make peace with?

For me, it was not waiting the doctors to tell me the whole story and me rushing out of that room. I now saw myself staying and connecting with my siblings, us going in together so that I had support from others. I could come to terms with what happened.

Rewrite how you want the dream to go. The more times you do this, giving the nightmare different ways to play out, will rewire your mind for the next time you fall asleep. Remember, dreams can be unpredictable. But by not eating too close to bedtime and watching a movie that gives you good feelings will help you to have positive reinforcements and lead to less distressing dreams.

Try other ways to help your rewrite to sink deeper into your mind. Try reading your revised script aloud first thing in the morning and just before you go to sleep. The brain loves repetition.

Your rewritten script needs to have enough detail that a stranger could read it and act it out. The clearer it reads, the easier your mind will turn it into a new memory. This new memory will be pulled into your mind when you're next dreaming. If you have many recurring nightmares, once you've cured the first nightmare, move onto the next. Chances are, however, your mind is now full of new positive memories.

Managing Stress

We are all imperfect people in an imperfect world

Conquering stress doesn't need to be stressful. You do not need to read pages and pages of how stress can make you feel terrible and how it can have a negative impact on your mind and body.

No matter how well we deal with our anxiety, at some point we will all go through stressful times in our lives. Making sure that we have the skills in place to help us cope with stress will help us to keep control of our anxiety levels.

Stress, like anxiety, can come from different sources. Some of these may be from social media, traffic on your way to work when you're already late, an upcoming exam or a bill that you've been putting off paying and now you've started to receive demand letters. Stress doesn't need to be one huge problem: it can be lots of small issues that build leaving you feeling overwhelmed and unable to cope.

We have already seen how stress causes hormones to be released, especially cortisol. This hormone not only causes us to feel terrible but also has a direct impact on our physical health too. You won't be surprised to learn that is can cause headaches, memory loss, disrupted sleep, high blood pressure, even putting you at a greater risk of heart attacks.

Have you ever been so stressed at work or cramming for an exam that you've picked up a cold that just can't shake off? This is down to the stress overworking the body and running our immune system down to the point where it can't fight off infections it normally would. Being stressed also releases adrenaline. Not so much that it causes us to panic but just enough to give us sore, aching muscles. These are all major warning signs that you're becoming very stressed and you need to take it easy. I know you need to work and you can't just take time off. Nor can you escape that exam that's looming; you need to study or how will you pass? You may feel like you can't rest until it's all done but taking time out will help you to be more focused and productive.

Try these simple suggestions to help you to wind down and recharge:

1. Take a hot bath or shower. This will help to soothe tight, aching muscles and will help to lift your mood. Think of it as a warming cuddle.

2. Try progressive muscle relaxation techniques. This can be as simple and scrunching up your feet and hands, holding for a few seconds, then releasing the tension. Or, if you are struggling to switch off in bed, start with squeezing up all the muscles on your face, holding for a second, then relaxing. Repeat this, moving down your body. You could even add in

guided meditation to help stop your mind overthinking.

3. Going for a stroll outdoors will give you a boost in endorphins and some much-needed vitamin D. Even 15–20 minutes is better than none. Turn your phone off or put it on silent so that you're not distracted.

4. Have a date night, either with a friend or a partner. Or a pamper night just for you! Watch a movie that makes you laugh and enjoy your favourite meal or snack. This will release the hormone oxytocin and give you that warm, fuzzy feeling.

5. Use an oil burner and add a few drops of camomile and lavender or other essential oils. Try and stay away from caffeine. This will lower your stress hormones and decrease your blood pressure.

6. Use box breathing whenever you feel you need to.

Digestive Issues

How to handle stomach problems

Did you know we have two brains?

The first is our central nervous system: our brain, spine and the nerves that connect to our body. The second is the enteric nervous system of the gut, made up of an extensive network of neurons that line the walls of the gastrointestinal tract.

Serotonin isn't just present in the brain. Our gut produces about 95% of the serotonin in the body. Changes to the levels in our brains have a direct impact on our digestive system. When there is an imbalance in the brain, it sends pulses down to our enteric system and causes things like butterflies or that feeling of dread in the bottom of our stomachs. In turn, this can cause us to suffer constipation, diarrhoea, pain, bloating and excessive wind. You may also experience nausea. It's important that we know that's there is a reason why our stomach reacts in the way that it does so that we can better prevent and treat issues. It is always worth getting any digestive issues checked out by your doctor.

I have Crohn's disease, which is part of the inflammatory bowel disease or IBD family of diseases. I know that if I don't manage my stress and anxiety levels, it can lead to a flare-up, leaving me stuck in the house for days. Stress can have an impact on acid from my stomach jumping up into my oesophagus, known as acid reflux. This can be incredibly painful and, before my diagnosis, I thought I was having a heart attack as the pain was in the middle of my chest.

The more we feel stressed, the more our body pumps out the hormones to get us to fight or run. This can be a circle of mental, emotional and physical pain. It is always wise to remember that taking medicine will help to relieve your symptoms but learning skills to manage your anxiety will help you to have more control.

Still not sure if your anxiety is causing digestive issues?

Another factor to think about is the bacteria that live in our gut and how they impact our bodies. Most of the bacteria live in our small and large intestines and help to keep our body functioning correctly. One of their jobs is to help our immune system. Studies have shown there are significant differences in people's gut health between people that suffer from anxiety and stress and those who don't.

Research conducted by the British Medical Journal reviewed 71 other studies that were published between 2003 and 2019. They looked at how prebiotics and probiotics may help adults with anxiety and depression. The team of researchers identified 7 studies showing huge improvements compared to people taking to treatment or a placebo.

Remember, if you can reduce or cut out sugar and processed foods, you will be helping your microbiome to recover and start to thrive. If you have gut issues, for example, you struggle to digest fibre and need to have a low residue diet, you can still get all the benefits from eating a colourful diet and taking probiotic supplements. I would highly recommend that you go to health food stores. They have staff trained in the different products available and they can help you choose products that will fit your lifestyle and budget and give you the benefits mentioned above.

Here are simple steps to help you to reach good gut health.

1. If you are suffering with intestinal issues, get it checked out. Your local chemist may be able to offer you over the counter medicine and further advice.

2. Use the skills you have already learnt in this guide to calm your anxiety and stress levels. This will help calm that anxious-tummy feeling.

3. Try taking processed foods out of your diet and replace them with foods that haven't been altered and can easily be found in nature.

4. Go to your local health store and speak to an adviser. If you feel unsure of this, look up some of the websites listed at the end of this book.

Conclusion

Now that you have learnt the key skills it's time to put everything you've learnt into action!

Sign your self-accountability contract and choose to live rather than just exist. Once I took responsibility for my circumstances, my life started to dramatically change. I finally felt free and in control of my life, rather than waiting and hoping that someone else would come along and save me. I realised that I am far more capable than I had ever realised.

Think of a time when you excelled at something. Everything just flowed and it was easy. It made you feel great and, for whatever reason, you stopped doing it. When you returned to it, you struggled. It felt unnatural and awkward but you knew that once you got back into it again great feelings would return. That's how these skills work. If you don't use them, you'll lose them. Just do one thing a day to practise.

Look at what you've been through. You've survived. Now it's time to live and let go of the things that have been holding you back. The past has been written but your future is free for you to write. You are now armed with the powerful skills that will develop your openness, courageousness and your spirit, allowing you to let go of all the lies you've told yourself and let go of your fear because when you do life will come flooding in ways that you never imagined possible!

Become your own superhero: the world is waiting for you.

Sending you love and light,

L Goodrick

Developing your Unique Steps

Making the skills your own

Take a deeper look into your own experiences and try the skills again but with these pointers in mind, you may discover something new.

Social Media Detox

1. Find ways to enrich other people's lives away from the online environment.

2. Make a list of the things you used to love doing and, for whatever reason, stopped. Reconnect with those activities and start putting them back into your life.

3. Start your detox small: stay off your devices for an hour, then the next day, try 3 hours. Cutting it out

straight away can increase your anxiety or loneliness, especially if you have a dependency on social media. Once you fill your time with meaningful interactions, the easier you'll find it.

4. Get more natural daylight. A screen's blue light can increase your serotonin levels. Being outdoors, you'll be getting the other benefits too, like vitamin D.

Letting go of Toxic Treats

1. Realise when you're having your toxic treat. Do you enjoy it or are you having it because it's easy?

2. Imagine how amazing you will feel when your habit no longer has power over you.

3. Take all the negativity out of your life for a week and see what positive changes occur. Try taking out social media or stop watching TV. Only let things into your life that serve you well. Rather than taking

in negative feelings, only take in the things that make you feel great.

4. Find a healthier alternative to the old toxic treat that nourishes your mind and body.

Disassociation

1. Find your pebble or trinket.

2. Take Charge. Reconnecting doesn't happen by chance; you can direct yourself out of being disconnected.

3. Trust in the process.

4. Have patience. It will become easy; you just need to practice.

Box Breathing

1. Take control of your anxiety levels and practise breathing so that you are prepared for when you need them the most.

2. Turn off the negative chatter and replace it with the positive feedback you got with the Who Am I? skill.

3. When you can't sleep go through your breathing and listen to a guided meditation.

4. When you're going into a new situation use box breathing to take stock of how you want your experience to be.

Reprogramming your Dreams

1. Find a piece of guided meditation music that helps you to feel comfortable.

2. Rehearse and relax first thing in the morning and right before bed.

3. Try using essential oils to help you enter a calm state before sleep.

4. Try and limit anything negative 1–2 hours before bed. Instead, choose something that makes you laugh and feel good.

Who am I?

1. Surround yourself with others that love and support you. Feel their love and respect and enjoy this feeling.

2. Show others your gratitude and make them feel good. What you put out to the world you attract back.

3. Allow others to see you, as you see yourself. This will give them permission to help you more.

4. Remember the negatives are just chances to improve yourself. Allow yourself to become a more rounded person.

Managing Stress

1. Find ways that you can take short 20-minute breaks throughout your day.

2. Try and have a balance in your life; whatever you are doing, make sure you take time out to relax.

3. Take up a new hobby and socialise more.

4. Learn to say no: don't overstretch yourself.

Digestive Issues

1. Look into an anti-inflammatory nutrition plan that can help ease pre-existing conditions.

2. Speak to a nutritionist, ideally one that specialises in holistic approaches.

3. Do further research to find the right balance for you.

4. If you have had gut issues before your anxiety started, make sure to get this checked out. Ask your doctor to run a faeces sample just to put your mind at ease to rule out anything that could be causing your issues.

Helpful Stuff

Podcasts and Guided Meditations

I've included some of my favourite podcasts and guided meditation links so that you have a starting point. Once you get a feel for what is good for you, you'll be able to find your own. All these links have totally free to access.

These are here to assist you to find what feels right for you. These all reinforce a positive state.

If you feel you would like to increase your vibration or have a greater understanding of your own spirituality journey, I highly recommend Angelina she will help you to develop your own connection to your higher power and will help you to shine greater than the sun.

She is a qualified counsellor with an HPD qualification, BACP accredited and specialises in life coaching.
You can contact her at,
Web Page www.counsellingandhealth.com
Email: angelina@counsellingandhealth.com

I am in no way affiliated with or connected to any of these below companies or organisations These are some of the resources that work for me and I hope they work for you too.

These are all on Instagram, iTunes and Spotify. They are all beautiful and true productions that reinforce positive vibes into your mind:

1. *The Nutrition & Mindset Podcast* with Jake Murphy
2. *Impact Theory* with Tom Bilyeu
3. *Mind Valley* with Vishen Lakhiani
4. *Think Biblically* with Scott Rae and Sean McDowell

Nutritional and Supplement Information and Companies

www.nutrition.bmj.com

www.nhs.uk/live-well/eat-well

www.healthnotes.online

www.avogel.co.uk

www.solgar.com

www.naturesaid.co.uk

YouTube Meditations

10 minutes – https://youtu.be/hKS1SG_PZD0 – by Declutter The Mind

20 minutes – https://youtu.be/jobVHhlMmRo – by The Honest Guys

30 minutes – https://youtu.be/d8AsVMvbIKE – by Caroline McCready

45 minutes – https://youtu.be/D9tLtmBlodg – by Jess Shepherd at Rising Higher Meditation

Also by Jess Shepherd is the sleep meditation below which I love! The recordings last for 8 hours and are brilliant to play while you sleep: https://youtu.be/DAJryaxrmg4

Do not listen to any meditation tracks while driving or operating machinery.

Additional Reading

Break Free from the Suffering Cycle of Abuse by L Goodrick

The Low GL Diet Bible by Patrick Holford

The Power of Now by Eckhart Tolle

Good Sugar Bad Sugar by Allen Carr

As a Man Thinketh and *As a Woman Thinketh* by James Allen

How to Stop Emotional Flashbacks by Richard Grannon

Rewire your brain to break your bad habits by Richard O'Connor

The surprisingly dramatic role of nutrition in mental health by Julia Rucklidge, TEDx Christian Church

www.patrickhollford.com - Health Advice | Nutrition Advice

www.foodforthebrain.org – Why is nutrition important to the brain?

www.bebrainfit.com -The brain benefits of the omega 3.

www.iflscience.com – 7 nutrients important to mental health and where to find them.

www.health.harvard.edu/blog/omega-3-fatty-acids-for-mood-disorders-2018080314414

TEDx Tyson, Quit social media by Dr C Newport

Charities

www.samaritans.org or call 116 123.

www.ageuk.org.uk 0800 678 1602

www.anxietyuk.org.uk 03444 775 774

www.supportline.org.uk 01708 765 200

Acknowledgements

This book is dedicated to every single survivor. No matter how alone or isolated you have felt, know that nothing lasts forever.

To all that have fallen victim to procrastination and self-sabotaging habits and to anyone that has lost their love for themselves.

To every human being that has felt lost in this world and exists from day to day, waiting for the next something to hurt them or scare them in some way.

This book is to assist *you* to find who you. To become the amazing person, you have always known yourself to be, brave and courageous.

Make a choice and your greatness will follow.

Special Thanks to

God. You are my strength when I was weak. You saw the best in me, and You showed me my purpose. No matter how hard I pushed You away, You never left me.

Elizabeth Brown for supporting me through my most challenging and darkest days. When my anxiety was at its worse, you were an amazing person, and I was lucky to have you as a friend.

Mr and Mrs Wood, anyone that crosses your path you show love and compassion to. You were there anytime I needed love and light. You were always there, no matter what. I can't put into words just how much you meant to me.

Danni James, you are an incredible lady. You give your everything to anyone that needs help, without questioning or judgement. You are a beacon of hope. You showed me great kindness and taught me lessons.

My sister and her family for taking me in when I had nowhere else to go. You showed me love and kindness.

Leanne White, reminding me why I started this journey and to keep going no matter what.

Nicholas Taylor, my editor for making my words flow so my books may help the people that need to hear that they are incredible and that they are not alone.

If I can be involved in anyway spreading light and love into yours or others lives, please email me: LG.breakfree@gmail.com or find me on Instagram: @breakfree.lg

Disclaimer

Although every effort was made to ensure that the information in this book was correct at the time of press, the author does not assume and hereby denies any liability to any party for any loss, damage or disruption caused by errors or omissions, whether such errors or omissions result from negligence, accident or any other cause. This book is not intended as a substitute for the medical advice of physicians. The reader should regularly consult physicians relating to their health, in particular to any symptoms that may require diagnosis or medical attention. I advise readers to take full responsibility for their safety and know their limits before practising the skills described in this book. At any point, if you feel unsure, take action and speak to a healthcare professional.

References

Allan Schore, 'Dr. Allan Schore on the Physiological Impact of Dissociation' [video], *PsychAlive* (08/05/2014), https://www.psychalive.org/video-dr-allan-schore-physiological-impact-dissociation/, accessed 19/03/2021

Ana Sandoiu, 'Vitamin D and brain health: New mechanism may explain link', *Medical News Today* (25/02/2019), accessed 19/03/2021

'Can Anxiety or Stress Cause a Heart Attack?', Study.com (28/04/2016), study.com/academy/lesson/can-anxiety-or-stress-cause-a-heart-attack.html, accessed 19/03/2021

Caroline McCready Meditation, '30 Minute Guided Breathing Meditation for Inner Calm and Depp Stillness' [video], YouTube (12/05/2020), https://youtu.be/d8AsVMvbIKE, accessed 19/03/2021

Casey Newton, 'There's more evidence Facebook can make you feel lonely', The Verge (13/11/2018), https://www.theverge.com/2018/11/13/18090016/facebook-study-loneliness-depression-hunt-pennsylvania, accessed 19/03/2021

'Complex PTSD – Post-traumatic stress disorder', *NHS* (last reviewed 27/09/2018), https://www.nhs.uk/mental-health/conditions/post-traumatic-stress-disorder-ptsd/complex/, accessed 19/03/2021

David Mischoulon, 'Omega-3 fatty acids for mood disorders', Harvard Medical School (27/10/2020), https://www.health.harvard.edu/blog/omega-3-fatty-acids-for-mood-disorders-2018080314414, accessed 19/03/2021

Declutter The Mind, '10 Minute Guided Meditation for PTSD (No Music, Voice Only) [video], YouTube (11/09/2020), https://youtu.be/hKS1SG_PZD0, accessed 19/03/2021

Demystifying Medicine, 'Abnormal psychology professor explains dissociative identity disorder (DID)' [video], YouTube (10/04/2019), https://www.youtube.com/watch?v=wIiFTXXkDTo, accessed 19/03/2021

'Dialectical Behavior Therapy', *Behavioral Research & Therapy Clinics, University of Washington,* https://depts.washington.edu/uwbrtc/about-us/dialectical-behavior-therapy/, accessed 19/03/2021

'Dissociative disorders', *NHS* (last reviewed 10/08/2020), https://www.nhs.uk/mental-health/conditions/dissociative-disorders/, accessed 19/03/2021

Eliot R. Smith, Diane M. Mackie, Heather M. Claypool, 'Social Psychology: Fourth Edition' (2004)

Herbert S. Ormsbee, III, Joseph D. Fondacaro, 'Action of serotonin on the gastrointestinal tract.' *Proceedings of the Society for Experimental Biology and Medicine* 178.3 (1985): 333-338, https://journals.sagepub.com/doi/abs/10.3181/00379727-178-42016, accessed 19/03/2021

Jacob F. Collen, Christopher J. Lettieri, Monica Hoffman, 'The Impact of Posttraumatic Stress Disorder on CPAP Adherence in Patients with Obstructive Sleep Apnea', *Journal of Clinical Sleep Medicine*, 08 (2012), https://jcsm.aasm.org/doi/full/10.5664/jcsm.2260, accessed 19/03/2021

Jake Murphy, 'The Nutrition and Mindset Podcast' [podcast series], Spotify (May 2020 to September 2020), https://open.spotify.com/show/6S0GZ31GqzmZVp DNv51hKb?si=vDNWAyChT_ust_GzAAY7gA&n d=1, accessed 19/03/2021

James L. Wilson, 'Stress, Cortisol and the Immune System: What Makes Us Get Sick?', AdrenalFatigue (24/09/2014), https://adrenalfatiguae.org/stress-cortisol-and-the-immune-system-what-makes-us-get-sick/, accessed 19/03/2021

Jess Shephard, Rising Higher Meditation, 'Extremely Powerful Guided Meditation to Manifest Your Dreams and Desires' [video], YouTube (15/07/2019), https://youtu.be/D9tLtmBlodg, accessed 19/03/2021

Joanne L. Davis, Jamie L. Rhudy, Kristi E. Pruiksma, Patricia Byrd, Amy E. Williams, Klanci M. McCabe, Emily J. Bartley, 'Physiological predictors of response to exposure, relaxation, and rescripting therapy for chronic nightmares in a randomized clinical trial', *Journal of Clinical Sleep Medicine* 7.6 (2011): 622-631, https://jcsm.aasm.org/doi/full/10.5664/jcsm.1466, accessed 19/03/2021

Joshua Z. Rosenthal, Sarina Grosswald, Richard Ross, Norman Rosenthal, 'Effects of Transcendental Meditation in Veterans of Operation Enduring

Freedom and Operation Iraqi Freedom With Posttraumatic Stress Disorder: A Pilot Study', Military Medicine, Volume 176, Issue 6, June 2011, Pages 626–630, https://doi.org/10.7205/MILMED-D-10-00254

Julia J Rucklidge, 'The surprisingly dramatic role of nutrition in mental health' [video], TEDx Christchurch (10/11/2014), https://www.tedxchristchurch.com/julia-rucklidge, accessed 19/03/2021

Keisha Findley, David R. Williams, Elizabeth A. Grice and Vence L. Bonham, 'Health Disparities and the Microbiome', *Trends in Microbiology* (November 2016), https://scholar.harvard.edu/files/davidrwilliams/files/findley_et_al._health_disparities_and_the_microbiome_2016.pdf, accessed 19/03/2021

M. Head, L. Goodwin, F. Debell, N. Greenberg, S. Wessely & N. T. Fear, 'Post-traumatic stress disorder and alcohol misuse: comorbidity in UK military personnel', *Soc Psychiatry Psychiatr Epidemiol* 51, 1171–1180 (2016) https://doi.org/10.1007/s00127-016-1177-8, accessed 19/03/2021

Marsha M. Linehan, 'DBT Skills Training Handouts and Worksheets, Second Edition: Nightmare Protocol, Step by Step', https://depts.washington.edu/uwbrtc/wp-content/uploads/Nightmare-Protocol.pdf, accessed 19/03/2021

Moira Burke, Cameron Marlow, Thomas M Lento, 'Social network activity and social well-being', *Proceedings of the SIGCHI Conference on Human Factors in Computing Systems* (April 2010),

175

https://dl.acm.org/doi/10.1145/1753326.1753613, accessed 19/03/2021

Patrick Holford, 'The Optimum Nutrition Bible' (2004)

Richard Grannon, 'How to Deal With PTSD, 3 Practical Tips' [video], YouTube (18/07/2016), https://www.youtube.com/watch?v=6rAInx1zG48, accessed 19/03/2021

Sanjay Noonan, Meena Zaveri, Elaine Macaninch3 and Kathy Martyn, 'Food & mood: a review of supplementary prebiotic and probiotic interventions in the treatment of anxiety and depression in adults', *BMJ Nutrition, Prevention & Health* (2020): bmjnph-2019, https://nutrition.bmj.com/content/early/2020/11/05/bmjnph-2019-000053.abstract, accessed 19/03/2021

Sean McDowell and Scott Rae, 'Think Biblically' [podcast series], Spotify (October 2017 to present), https://open.spotify.com/show/4gZECpHCBwJXXF3B6INcmw?si=3W1F2OJmR3aFfaf1HI08KA&nd=1, accessed 19/03/2021

TEDx Talks, 'Quit social media | Dr. Cal Newport | TEDxTysons' [video], YouTube (19/09/2016), https://www.youtube.com/watch?v=3E7hkPZ-HTk, accessed 19/03/2021

'The Brain-Gut Connection', *Johns Hopkins Medicine* (n.d.), https://www.hopkinsmedicine.org/health/wellness-and-prevention/the-brain-gut-connection, accessed 19/03/2021

The Honest Guys, 'Mindfulness Meditation – Guided 20 Minutes' [video], YouTube (09/01/2018), https://youtu.be/jobVHhlMmRo, accessed 19/03/2021

Tom Bilyeu, 'Impact Theory' [podcast series], Spotify (January 2017 to present), https://open.spotify.com/show/1nARKz2vTIOb7gC 9dusE4b?si=bAYCsH13Swa32A2eIrz-ww&nd=1, accessed 19/03/2021

Tracey L.Biehn, Ateka Contractor, Jon D. Elhai, Marijo Tamburrino, Thomas H. Fine, Marta R. Prescott, EdwinShirley, Philip K. Chan, Renee Slembarski, Israel Liberzon, Joseph R. Calabrese, Sandro Galea, 'Relations between the underlying dimensions of PTSD and major depression using an epidemiological survey of deployed Ohio National Guard soldiers. Journal of affective disorders', *Journal of Affective Disorders* 144: 106-111 (2013), https://www.sciencedirect.com/science/article/abs/p ii/S0165032712004624, accessed 19/03/2021

'Types of PTSD', *PsychCentral* (last reviewed 17/05/2016), https://psychcentral.com/lib/types-of-ptsd, accessed 19/03/2021

University of Georgia, 'Vitamin D deficiency, depression linked in international study', *ScienceDaily* (02/12/2014), https://www.sciencedaily.com/releases/2014/12/141 202111148.htm, accessed 19/03/2021

US National Library of Medicine, 'Omega-3 Fatty Acids and Post Traumatic Stress Disorder (PTSD)' (2010), https://clinicaltrials.gov/ct2/show/NCT00644423, accessed 19/03/2021

Vishen Lakhiani, 'The Mindvalley Podcast' [podcast series], Spotify (November 2017 to present), https://open.spotify.com/show/33x8LqNwzBthoVa3 im6NdO?si=JswyjbtmQvGRVchz7WxOnw&nd=1, accessed 19/03/2021

Printed in Great Britain
by Amazon